GREEK MYTHOLOGY

ATHENA

BY WHITNEY SANDERSON

CONTENT CONSULTANT
ALISON C. TRAWEEK, PhD
ADJUNCT INSTRUCTOR OF GREEK AND ROMAN CLASSICS
TEMPLE UNIVERSITY

An Imprint of Abdo Publishing
abdobooks.com

abdobooks.com

Printed in the United States of America, North Mankato, Minnesota.
102021
012022

THIS BOOK CONTAINS RECYCLED MATERIALS

Cover Photo: Shutterstock Images
Interior Photos: iStockphoto, 4–5, 6, 10, 28 (bottom); Shutterstock Images, 7, 16, 26; Mondadori Portfolio/Hulton Fine Art Collection/Getty Images, 8; IMG Stock Studio/Shutterstock Images, 12–13; Ashmolean Museum University of Oxford/Heritage Images/Hulton Archive/Getty Images, 14, 28 (top); Hoika Mikhail/Shutterstock Images, 19, 29 (top); The Picture Art Collection/Alamy, 20, 29 (bottom); Pictures Now/Universal Images Group North America LLC/Alamy, 22–23; North Wind Picture Archives/AP Images, 24

Editor: Alyssa Sorenson
Series Designer: Ryan Gale

Library of Congress Control Number: 2021941254

Publisher's Cataloging-in-Publication Data

Names: Sanderson, Whitney, author.
Title: Athena / by Whitney Sanderson
Description: Minneapolis, Minnesota : Abdo Publishing, 2022 | Series: Greek mythology | Includes online resources and index.
Identifiers: ISBN 9781532196751 (lib. bdg.) | ISBN 9781098218560 (ebook)
Subjects: LCSH: Athena (Greek deity)--Juvenile literature. | Mythology, Greek--Juvenile literature. | Gods, Greek--Juvenile literature.
Classification: DDC 292--dc23

CONTENTS

The city of Athens, Greece, has been around for thousands of years. It was named after Athena.

ATHENA'S CITY

The goddess Athena stood on a rocky ledge. Her armor shone in the sunlight. She watched the city below. The people there were hard workers. They grew crops from the stony soil. There were many fine artists. The soldiers were brave and strong.

Athena is one of the most well-known Greek goddesses.

Many people know Poseidon as the god of the sea. But he is also the god of horses and earthquakes.

Athena decided it was a worthy place. She wanted to be the city's **patron** goddess. Then it would take her name. The people would build a **temple** for her. Only one obstacle stood in her way. Poseidon, the god of the sea, wanted the city for himself.

Athena and Poseidon agreed to hold a contest. Each would give the city a gift. The people would then pick who was most worthy to lead them.

Athena, *bottom right*, and Poseidon, *bottom left*, were two of the 12 major Olympian gods.

Poseidon raised his golden **trident** high. He hit it against the ground. A spring of water bubbled forth. At first, the people cheered in amazement. Then a man stepped forward and brought a handful of the water to his lips. He quickly spit it out. The water was as salty as the ocean Poseidon ruled.

Athena struck her spear into the earth. A green shoot sprouted from the ground. Soon, it became a fully grown olive tree. The tree's wood could be used for fuel and shelter. Its fruit could be eaten and pressed to make oil.

Greek Myths

Ancient Greeks believed some gods or goddesses could control different parts of nature, such as the weather or the sea. Some had power over parts of human life, such as childbirth, hunting, or war. The ancient Greeks told stories called myths about their gods and goddesses.

Ancient Greeks were known for their artwork, including the statues they had on buildings.

The tree's leaves offered shade from the summer sun. The people agreed that Athena's gift was the most useful. From that day forward, the city would be called Athens.

Who Were the Ancient Greeks?

The ancient Greek **civilization** existed more than 2,000 years ago. It was in southeastern Europe. The city of Athens was at the heart of ancient Greece. The Greeks believed in many different gods and goddesses. Athena was the goddess of war and wisdom. She was also known for her crafting skills, such as weaving.

Further Evidence

Look at the website below. Does it give any new evidence to support Chapter One?

Athena

abdocorelibrary.com/athena

Zeus was one of the strongest Greek gods.

ANCIENT STORIES

Zeus was the king of the gods. He lived on Mount Olympus, high among the clouds. He controlled thunder and lightning. But there was a prophecy that said one day his own child would be more powerful than him. Zeus did not want to give up his place.

Throughout the years, people have made artwork showing Athena's birth.

Zeus's wife Metis was a Titan goddess. When Zeus found out that Metis was expecting a child, he swallowed her up. Soon, Zeus's head began to ache. A short time later, Athena sprang from Zeus's forehead. She was fully grown and wearing armor.

Titans and Olympians

The Titans were a group of gods. Zeus's parents were Titans. His father was king of the Titans. Zeus decided to overthrow him. Zeus and his siblings battled the Titans for a long time. They won and formed a new family of gods called the Olympians.

Different cities in ancient Greece often fought each other. Many people hoped Athena was on their side.

War, Justice, and Inventions

Athena and her half brother Ares were the goddess and god of war. However, while Ares was hot tempered, Athena was calm and rational. She believed war should be used as a tool for justice. Some versions of Athena's story say her closest friend was Nike, the goddess of victory. Because Athena usually won her battles, they spent a lot of time together.

Battle was not Athena's only interest. She was an inventor too. Some stories say she created the chariot, the plow, and the **bridle**. She had a special way with horses. That may be why so many of the things she invented used horsepower.

Athena and Arachne

Athena was known for her skill at weaving. Like her father, Athena could be proud and jealous. Once, Athena overheard a young woman named Arachne say her own weaving was better than Athena's.

The goddess and the young woman challenged each other to a weaving contest. Some stories say that Athena got jealous over how perfect Arachne's tapestry was. Athena turned the woman into the greatest spinner of all—a spider.

Athena the Wise

Most of the time, Athena was a fair goddess. She was known for her wisdom and good advice.

Athena helped Odysseus on his dangerous journey.

She protected the hero Odysseus as he traveled from Troy to his home in Ithaca. She helped other heroes such as Jason, Hercules, and Perseus on their **quests** too.

Athena put Medusa's head on her shield.

For instance, Perseus needed to slay a snake-headed monster named Medusa. But anyone who looked at Medusa turned to stone. In one version of the story, Athena gave Perseus a shield that reflected like a mirror. Perseus was able to keep an eye on Medusa's reflection without looking directly at her. This helped him slay the monster. Perseus eventually gave Medusa's head to Athena.

Athena never married, but she adopted a son named Erechtheus. He became the king of Athens. He created a festival called the Panathenaea. Every four years, the city came alive with music, dancing, and athletic games in Athena's honor.

Explore Online

Visit the website below. Does it give any new information about Greek mythology that wasn't in Chapter Two?

What Is Greek Mythology?

abdocorelibrary.com/athena

Athena was a smart, brave goddess.

CHAPTER 3

ATHENA IN GREECE

Athena was an important goddess to the ancient Greeks. They were often at war, either among themselves or with other civilizations, such as the Persians. Training for battle was a part of daily life.

People prayed to Athena. They wanted her to help them win battles.

Athena was known for her skills in arts and crafts as well as in war. Many works of art were made with Athena's image. These include paintings, weavings, sculptures, vases, and coins. Athena is usually shown as being tall and athletic. She often wears armor, such as a helmet. Athena usually has a shield and spear too.

Athena is often shown with several animals. One is an owl, which is a **symbol** of wisdom. Another is a serpent, which is a symbol of good judgment.

Pallas Who?

In some ancient Greek poems, Athena is called Pallas Athena. **Historians** are not sure exactly what *Pallas* means. It may be a word for "maiden." Or it may mean "to wave a spear." It could also be the name of a creature that appeared in some myths with Athena.

Map of Ancient Greece

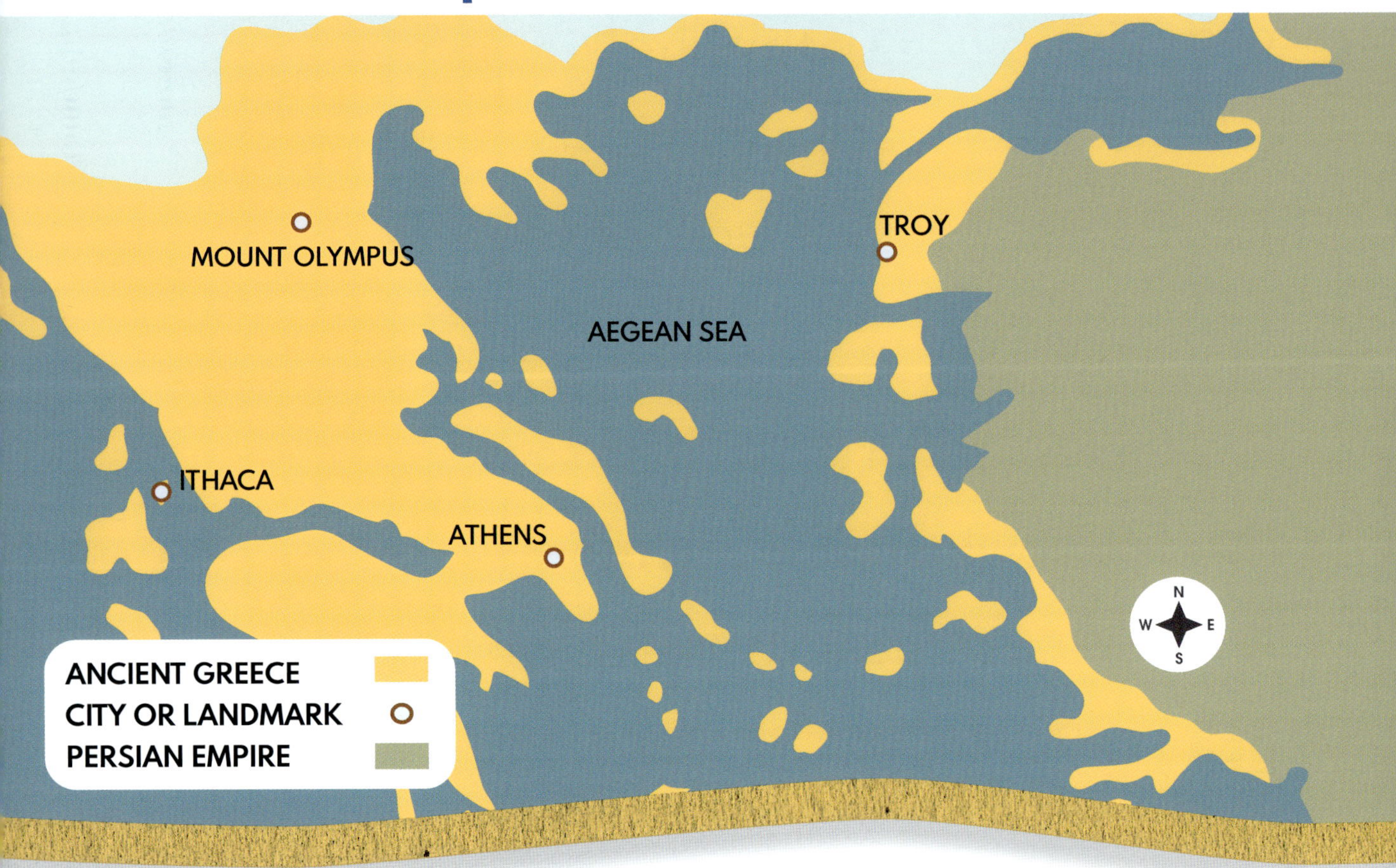

Ancient Greece was bigger than the country of Greece today. Its borders changed over time as the ancient Greeks won and lost wars.

Temple of the Goddess

The ancient Greeks built a famous temple for Athena. It is called the Parthenon. Visitors can see it today. It reminds people that Athens is still Athena's city.

PRIMARY SOURCE

Some ancient Greek hymns, or songs of praise, focus on Athena. One of them may have been written in the 600s BCE. It says:

> Of Pallas Athena, guardian of the city, I begin to sing. . . . It is she who saves the people as they go out to war and come back.

Source: "To Athena." *Perseus Digital Library*, n.d., perseus.tufts.edu. Accessed 21 May 2021.

Comparing Texts

Think about the quote. Does it support the information in this chapter? Or does it give a different perspective? Explain how in a few sentences.

LEGENDARY FACTS

Athena was the daughter of Zeus, the king of the gods, and Metis, a Titan goddess.

Athena was the Greek goddess of wisdom and war, and she was known for her skills with crafting.

Athena gave advice to Greek heroes and helped them on their quests.

Athena is said to have invented the chariot, the plow, and the bridle.

Glossary

bridle
a harness that is placed on a horse's head and is used to control or guide the animal

civilization
a society that's organized and developed

historians
people who study the past

patron
someone who is chosen as a special protector, guardian, or supporter

quests
journeys to do important tasks

symbol
something that represents a certain quality or idea

temple
a building used for worship

trident
a spear with three prongs

Online Resources

To learn more about Athena, visit our free resource websites below.

Visit **abdocorelibrary.com** or scan this QR code for free Common Core resources for teachers and students, including vetted activities, multimedia, and booklinks, for deeper subject comprehension.

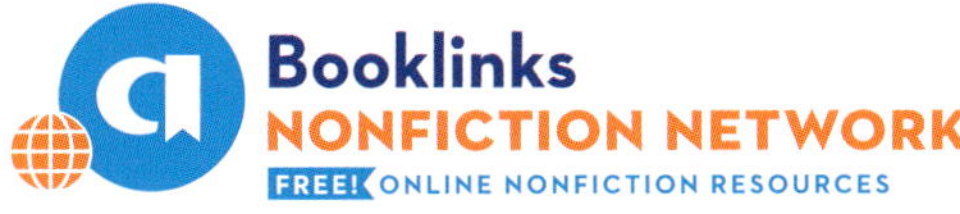

Visit **abdobooklinks.com** or scan this QR code for free additional online weblinks for further learning. These links are routinely monitored and updated to provide the most current information available.

Learn More

Greenberg, Imogen. *Athena: Goddess of Wisdom and War*. Amulet Books, 2021.

Hudak, Heather C. *Poseidon*. Abdo, 2022.

Sullivan, Laura L. *Pallas Athena*. Cavendish Square, 2020.

Index

About the Author

Whitney Sanderson is the author of numerous books for young readers, including five in the historical fiction series *Horse Diaries* and two in the history series *Events that Changed America*. She lives with her family in Massachusetts.